Remember Me

A book all about...

____

Dear Cancer Warrior,

These pages belong to you. You don't have to be profound. You don't have to find the perfect words. You don't even have to finish every page.

Draw something ridiculous. Circle an answer. Add a photograph. Make a list. Scribble in the corner. Stick something here that makes absolutely no sense to anyone but you.

There are no rules. This isn't about creating a perfect record of your life. It's about leaving behind something real. Something that feels like you.

You are greatly loved and you will be remembered forever.

Cancer may be part of your story, but it does not get to be the whole story. Before diagnoses, treatments, scans, hospitals, medicines, and medical words you probably never wanted to learn, there was you. And there is still you.

Your personality. Your dreams. Your favorite things. Your people. Your memories. Your opinions. Your sense of humor. The things you love and the things you definitely do not. Those things belong in your story too.

Especially those things.

People may have called you brave, strong, courageous, inspirational, or a warrior. Maybe sometimes those words feel good. Maybe sometimes they don't.

In these pages, you don't have to be any of those things. You can be funny. Angry. Hopeful. Scared. Sarcastic. Grateful. Tired. Happy. Sad. Loud. Quiet. Completely ridiculous.

You are allowed to simply be you. And that is enough.

You have already left footprints in this world. Some are big and easy to see. Others are so small you may not even know they are there. You have changed people simply because they have known you. You have been part of their stories, their memories, their laughter, and their lives.

There are people who will carry something they learned from you for the rest of their lives. That means a piece of you keeps traveling forward with them.

The Footprints I Leave

We all leave footprints behind. Not just the kind we make when we walk, but the invisible ones we leave on the hearts of the people who love us. Every laugh, every hug, every adventure, every ordinary day, and every moment of love leaves a little mark that says, "I was here."

Now you can create a footprint your family can keep forever.

Create Your Footprint

On a separate piece of heavy paper or canvas, create your own footprint. You can paint the bottom of your foot and gently press it onto the paper. Trace around your foot. Make a print using the bottom of your favorite shoe. Ask someone you love to help if doing it yourself is difficult. Then make it completely yours. Add your name or signature. Draw tiny hearts. Add your fingerprints. Write a few favorite words. Let the people you love add their fingerprints around yours. Or simply leave your footprint exactly as it is.

When it is finished, place it in a frame. Someday, the people you love can look at it and remember something very important:
You walked through this world.
You walked through their lives.
And you left footprints on their hearts that will always remain.

EXTRA:
Put your footprint in the center and have family members place a thumbprint heart around it.
Add words like "I was here. I was loved. I made a difference." at the bottom of the framed piece.

Colors of Me

Every color tells a story,
every shade a piece of me
the love I gave, the joy I found,
the person I chose to be.

I've colored these hearts with all that I am,
every bright and beautiful hue.
For the colors that filled my life with love
will live on in all of you.

A Little Piece of Me

A little piece of who I am,
a tiny treasure held in hand.
A piece of laughter, love, or glee,
a little memory made by me.
Keep it close and you will see
it holds a little piece of me.

A Little Piece of Me

We all have pieces of our story that words can't always explain. This is a place to leave a little piece of you behind.

How to Use This Envelope:

- ♡ Choose something small that means a lot to you.
- ♡ It could be a photo, a ticket, a tiny note, a pressed flower, a bracelet thread, a drawing, or anything else that tells a piece of your story.
- ♡ Place it inside the envelope below.
- ♡ This piece of you can be kept, remembered, and treasured forever.

My Constellation

Every person that I love
is a little star above.
Some shine softly, some shine bright,
each one filling up my life.
Connect the stars and you will see
all the love surrounding me.
And wherever your journey may start,
we'll always share the same sky in our hearts.

Scan the QR code to listen to the above song and remember that kids with cancer shine like stars in the midnight sky, filling the darkness with great sparkly light.

My Constellation ♡

Every star represents someone or something
that is important to you.
They brighten your life in their own way.
You can connect the stars however you choose!

You are part of so many stories, hearts, and lives.
You make the world a more beautiful place. ♡

The people we love become part of who we are, and that does not end when they are no longer with us. We remember their laughter, their favorite things, the stories they told, the things that made them happy, and the little moments that once seemed ordinary but become priceless with time.

Memories allow love to continue to be spoken, shared, and carried forward. Remembering someone is a way of saying, **"Your life mattered. You were here. You are still part of us."**

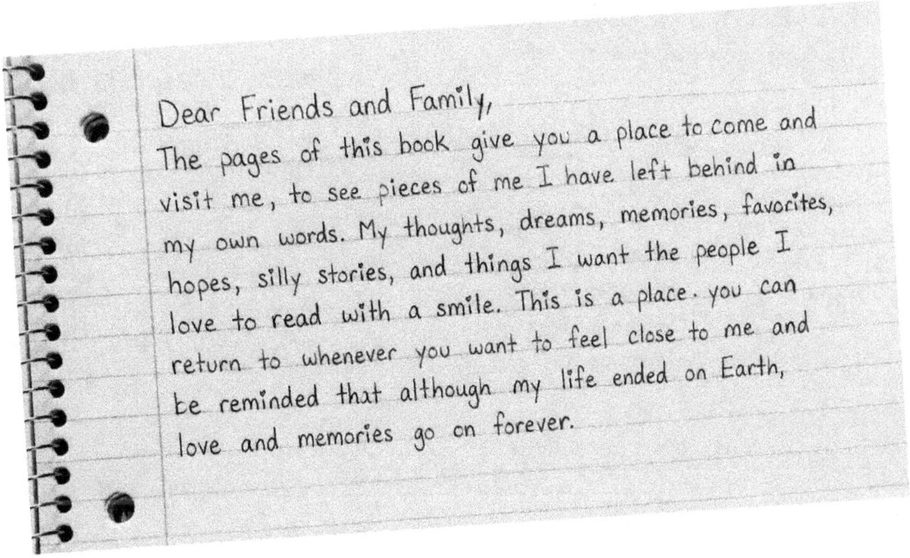

Dear Friends and Family,
The pages of this book give you a place to come and visit me, to see pieces of me I have left behind in my own words. My thoughts, dreams, memories, favorites, hopes, silly stories, and things I want the people I love to read with a smile. This is a place you can return to whenever you want to feel close to me and be reminded that although my life ended on Earth, love and memories go on forever.

my hopes and dreams

I may not get to see all of these come true, but dreaming is always free. ♡

the future me ♡

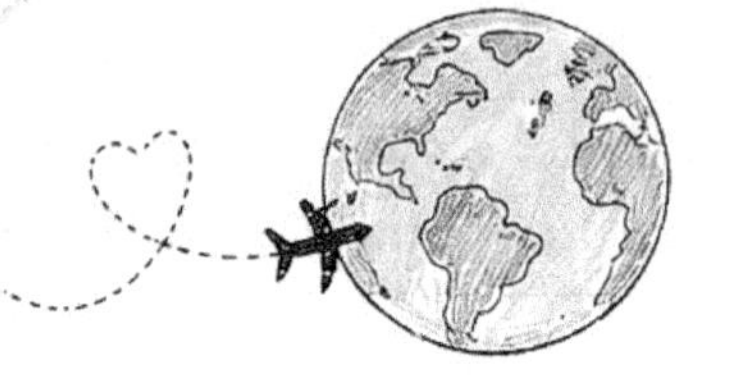

- I want to be happy.
- I want to inspire people.
  I want to make a difference.
- I want to live a life full of love and adventure. ♡

who I want to marry

I want a love that feels like home.

Kind
Funny
Loves Jesus
My best friend
Someone who will love me forever ♡

places I want to travel

- Italy ♡
- Hawaii
- Greece
- Bali ♡
- London
- Australia ♡
- New York City ♥

where I want to go to college ♡

- Somewhere with pretty trees and lots of sunshine
- A place where I can help others
- Maybe by the ocean?
- I want a close-knit community ♡

my dream job ♡

- Something creative
- Helping kids
- Writing books
- Or maybe a lawyer
- I just want to do something that matters. ♡

I want to leave little pieces of me everywhere I go. That's how I'll live forever. ♥

Even if I'm not here to see it,
I hope these dreams live on in the people I love. ♡

I may not have forever, but I have dreams worth holding onto. ♥

my hopes and dreams

I may not get to see all of these come true but dreaming is always free.

the future me

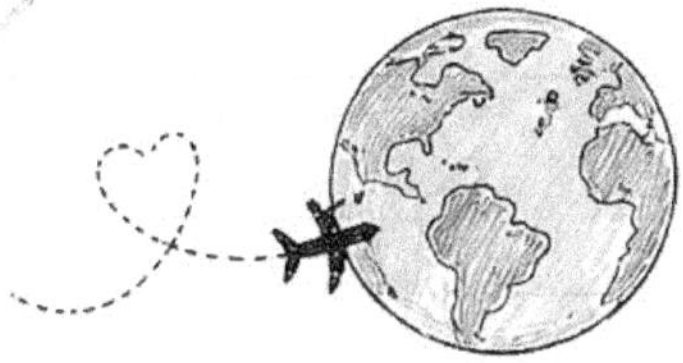

places I want to travel

who I want to marry

where I want to go to college

my dream job

I may not have forever, but I have dreams worth holding onto.

None of us lives forever. In this great race of life, we have a start line and a finish line. As I approach my finish line, I am feeling so much. Here are some of the things I'm feeling

In the pages of this book, you will read about me. You will read about my favorite things, my favorite places, my friends, my family, my hopes, and my dreams. You will read about my greatest passions and my wishes. You will read about the stuff I find funny and the stuff I think about when I'm sad. You will read about both my happy and sad moments. You will read about how I wish life could have been, but also about how I find joy in the present. Keep this book and remember me.

memories

My Favorites

My favorites

the things I love most ♡

favorite foods ♡

♡ ____________________
♡ ____________________
♡ ____________________
♡ ____________________
♡ ____________________
♡ ____________________
♡ ____________________
♡ ____________________
♡ ____________________

favorite colors ♡

♡ ____________________
♡ ____________________
♡ ____________________
♡ ____________________
♡ ____________________
♡ ____________________

favorite clothes & styles ♡

the outfits that make me feel like me.

comfortable, confident & completely me ♡

style is a way to say who you are without speaking. ♡

My favorite BOOKS & MOVIES

favorite books

the stories I love

- ______________________
- ______________________
- ______________________
- ______________________
- ______________________
- ______________________
- ______________________
- ______________________
- ______________________

favorite movies

the ones I could watch over and over

- ______________________
- ______________________
- ______________________
- ______________________
- ______________________
- ______________________
- ______________________
- ______________________
- ______________________

some movies make me laugh, some make me cry, and some stay with me forever.

the stories I love stay with me always.

my favorite CELEBRITIES & ACTIVITIES

favorite celebrities ♡

the people I look up to and admire ♡

- ____________________
- ____________________
- ♡ ____________________
- ♡ ____________________
- ♡ ____________________
- ♡ ____________________
- ♡ ____________________
- ♡ ____________________
- ♡ ____________________
- ♡ ____________________

favorite activities ♡

the things that make me happy and feel alive ♡

- ♡ ____________________
- ♡ ____________________
- ♡ ____________________
- ♡ ____________________
- ♡ ____________________
- ♡ ____________________
- ♡ ____________________
- ♡ ____________________
- ♡ ____________________
- ♡ ____________________

I don't just dream... I imagine, I plan, and I believe. ♡

dream big shine bright ♡

my favorite RESTAURANTS, FRIENDS, & ROOMS IN THE HOME

favorite restaurants ♥

the places that never disappoint ♥

♥ ______________________

♥ ______________________

♥ ______________________

♥ ______________________

♥ ______________________

♥ ______________________

favorite friends ♥

the people who make life better ♥

♥ ______________________

♥ ______________________

♥ ______________________

♥ ______________________

♥ ______________________

♥ ______________________

favorite rooms in the home ♥

the spaces that feel like me ♥

my bedroom

♥ ______________________

♥ ______________________

♥ ______________________

♥ ______________________

living room

♥ ______________________

♥ ______________________

♥ ______________________

♥ ______________________

kitchen

♥ ______________________

♥ ______________________

♥ ______________________

♥ ______________________

other favorite rooms

♥ ______________________

♥ ______________________

♥ ______________________

♥ ______________________

It's the people, the places, and the little things that make life so amazing. ♥

my favorite
VACATION SPOTS, SMELLS, & PETS

favorite vacation spots ♥

the places that take my breath away ♥

- ♥ ____________________
- ♥ ____________________
- ♥ ____________________
- ♥ ____________________
- ♥ ____________________
- ♥ ____________________
- ♥ ____________________

favorite smells ♥

the little things that make me smile ♥

- ♥ ____________________
- ♥ ____________________
- ♥ ____________________
- ♥ ____________________
- ♥ ____________________
- ♥ ____________________
- ♥ ____________________

favorite pets ♥

the furry (or not so furry) friends I love ♥

- ♥ ____________________
- ♥ ____________________
- ♥ ____________________
- ♥ ____________________
- ♥ ____________________
- ♥ ____________________

a place for all the cute faces ♥

Collect moments not things. ♥
They make the best memories. ♥

Sometimes we think the biggest moments are the ones people will remember most. But often, it is the little things. The sound of your laugh. The way you say someone's name. The song you always turn up too loud. Your favorite snack. The expression you make when someone annoys you. The silly joke you tell over and over. The way you hug someone you love. These tiny pieces of you may not seem important now. Someday, they may be priceless.

THE
little things
MATTER.
inside jokes
a kind message
favorite songs
the way someone makes me laugh
safe places
ordinary days become the best memories
dreams big and small

Memories are so important. Our experiences, both good and bad, shape us. They influence our life choices. We learn from the mistakes we make. Bad things that happen in our lives teach us how to be strong and confident.

Good things that happen are to be cherished memories. We should always be grateful for the happy moments and find joy in memories made with the ones we love.

Dear Loved Ones,
By sharing my memories with you, I'm sharing the real me. I'm sharing my joys and my sorrows because everything about me makes me me, and I want you to remember me the way I really am. My flaws and my quirks are part of me. Each moment in my life, however long it may last, holds meaning.

As you read through the next section, I hope you can picture me, feel my presence, laugh and cry, and close your eyes and remember me.

MEMORIES
S+T
S+T
SUMMER

my HAPPIEST MEMORY

the moment that made my heart the fullest

I want to remember this forever.
It will always make me smile.

The photo below is one I want you to look at often because it represents me when I'm happy. Remember me happy. Remember my smile and the light in my eyes. When you look at this picture, be happy. Remember me.

my SADDEST MEMORY

the moment that broke my heart ♡

It hurts to remember,
but I will never forget.
It made me who I am. ♡

We all get sad. It is ok to remember the sad times. And it's ok to be sad when I'm gone. You are allowed to cry. You are allowed to remember the sad times. Just remember to let those sad times build strength. Remember that I was sad sometimes, too, but I'm not sad now. I'm free. Remember me.

This is a photo of sad me

my FUNNIEST MEMORY

the moment that still makes me laugh ♥

LOL!

HA HA HA!

good times + silly moments = best memories ♥

Laughter is the best kind of memory to keep forever. ♥

Laughter is great medicine. When we laugh, we heal. That's why I want you to take a look at this photo of me and laugh. Laugh out loud! There might have been bad days, but do you know what else there were? Funny moments even on those bad days! So when you look at this photo of me, laugh! Laugh out loud and remember me.

Memories WITH FAMILY

the moments that mean the most ♡

Family is where
our story begins
and our memories
last forever. ♡

more Memories WITH FAMILY

making memories together

The best times are the ones we share together

This photo is our family, the way I see us in my mind. This is how I choose to remember us, and when you look at it, I hope you will love it like I love it. Take a nice, long look. Remember me.

This photo is one of us being goofy and I want you to look at this one and smile, remembering that not all the times were sad. We had funny ones too!

Memories WITH FRIENDS

the moments that mean the most ♡

BEST FRIENDS FOREVER ♡

GOOD TIMES ♡

MEMORIES

Friends make the good times better and the hard times easier. ♡

Friends! I will miss my friends so much, and I know they will miss me. See the photos below? That's how I want my friends to remember us together. I want them to be able to feel my presence even after I'm gone. Dear friends, remember me.

Memories WITH PETS

the moments that mean the most ♥

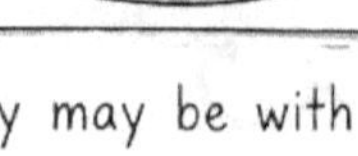

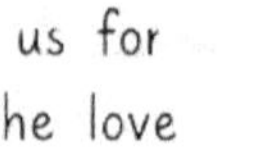

They may be with us for a short time, but the love they give lasts forever. ♥

My sweet “furever friends”, I love you, and I hope that when you smell something that belonged to me, you will happily remember me.

So Many THINGS to REMEMBER

Collect moments,
not things.

Read These and REMEMBER ME

Stories stay.
Memories live.
Love lasts forever.

Wishes

We all have hopes and dreams. We wish for life to be a certain way, but life rarely turns out the way any of us wishes it to be. These are some of the things I wish right now as I'm writing. Maybe some of these things will happen, and maybe they won't, but I want you to know what I wish, and when you read these next few pages, remember me.

My GREATEST WISHES

Dream big.
Believe in yourself
Anything is possible

101 Questions

My answers to 101 questions

1. Who is your favorite actor?

____

2. Who is your favorite musician?

____

3. What is your favorite song?

____

4. What is your favorite vacation spot?

____

5. If you had to choose,
would you live in the mountains or at the beach?

____

or

6. If you could visit any country
you've never been to, where would you go?

____

My answers to 101 questions

7. Who do you wish could be the president?

____

8. How tall are you?

____

9. What is your favorite color?

____

10. What is one of your biggest secrets?

____

11. If you were given one wish today, what would it be?

____

12. What color are your eyes?

____

13. If you could buy yourself one thing today, what would that be?

____

14. What would you do with $1 million if it were given to you right now?

____

15. What is your favorite piece of jewelry?

____

My answers to 101 questions

16. Who is your best friend?

____

17. What is your favorite nickname to be called?

____

18. Do you like sweet snacks or salty snacks?

____

19. What is your favorite "junk" food?

____

20. What is your favorite season?

____

21. Do you like snow?

____

22. What is one sport you wish you could try?

____

23. What is something you think you do well?

____

24. What is one thing you have never done that you wish you could do?

____

My answers to 101 questions

25. What do you think is your best physical feature?

____

26. Do you like to dance?

____

27. Do you like to sing?

____

28. Are you an introvert or an extrovert?

____

29. What is your "love language"?

____

30. What is your most embarrassing moment?

____

31. What item brings you the most comfort?

____

32. What is your favorite hobby?

____

33. What is your best talent?

____

My answers to 101 questions

34. Are you a book, movie, or podcast person?

35. If you could learn another language, which would it be?

36. What do you value most in a friendship?

37. What is something you believe in that not everyone does?

38. What legacy would you like to leave behind?

39. What is a risk you're glad you took?

40. What is your favorite way to spend a weekend?

41. Do you like coffee?

42. Do you prefer city life or country life?

My answers to 101 questions

43. Are you a morning person or night owl?

____

44. What is your favorite book?

____

45. What is one food you refuse to eat?

____

46. If you could be in any profession, what would you choose?

____

47. What is the most recent fact you learned?

____

48. Which room in the house makes you the happiest?

____

49. Who is your favorite athlete?

50. What is the best concert you've ever been to?

____

51. What is the hardest thing you ever had to do?

____

My answers to 101 questions

52. Do you like math?

____

53. Who is someone who has influenced you?

____

54. What childhood toy is your favorite?

____

55. How do you prefer to spend your free time?

____

56. Are you a planner or do you like to "go with the flow"?

____

57. If your life were a movie, what would it be called?

____

58. What is an accomplishment you're proud of?

____

59. If you could have dinner with a famous person, who would it be?

____

60. If you could have dinner with a fictional character, who would it be?

____

My answers to 101 questions

61. What does your dream house look like?

___

62. Do you sing in the shower?

___

63. Would you travel to space if you could?

___

64. Would you travel on a submarine if you could?

___

65. If you could switch places with someone for the day, who would it be?

___

66. Do you have a phobia?

___

67. Who is someone from the past you'd like to meet?

___

68. What is one dream you remember having?

___

69. If you could relive any single memory, what would it be?

___

My answers to 101 questions

70. What is your favorite city or town?

____

71. Who is your role model?

____

72. What is one of your biggest life lessons learned?

____

73. What is one characteristic you want people to remember about you?

____

74. Do you have a pet peeve?

____

75. What's your favorite cartoon character?

____

76. What do you think your friends would say is your greatest talent?

____

77. Would you rather lay on a blanket on a beach or sit by a campfire in the woods?

____

My answers to 101 questions

78. What is your favorite holiday?

____

79. What's your favorite app or website?

____

80. What's your favorite place to go shopping?

____

81. What is your favorite game to play?

____

82. What is your dream car?

____

83. What is your favorite animal?

____

84. What personality trait do you value?

____

85. What (or who) makes you laugh?

____

86. What makes you sad?

____

My answers to 101 questions

87. What is a cause you deeply believe in?

____

88. Do you like celebrating birthdays?

____

89. Do you know how to roller skate?

____

90. What is one word that describes you best?

____

91. Do you have a favorite teacher, boss or leader?

____

92. What is your favorite vacation?

____

93. Where is your least favorite place to go?

____

94. What is the worst food you ever ate?

____

95. Do you like cooking or having someone cook for you?

____

My answers to 101 questions

96. What was the happiest day of your life?

____

97. What surprise in your life made you the happiest?

____

98. When you think of the word "love", what do you picture?

____

99. What makes you feel peace?

____

100. What makes you feel excited?

____

101. What motivates you to try hard and not give up?

____

Let's Get to Know YOU!

Now that you've shared 101 things about yourself, interview your family and friends and ask them to describe you using only one word. Record their responses below.

NAME	ONE WORD TO DESCRIBE YOU

THANK YOU!

YOU ARE AMAZING!

Let's Get to Know YOU!

Now that you've shared 101 things about yourself, interview your family and friends and ask them to describe you using only one word. Record their responses below.

NAME	ONE WORD TO DESCRIBE YOU

THANK YOU!

YOU ARE AMAZING!

Let's Get to Know YOU!

Now that you've shared 101 things about yourself, interview your family and friends and ask them to describe you using only one word. Record their responses below.

NAME	ONE WORD TO DESCRIBE YOU

THANK YOU!

YOU ARE AMAZING!

Druthers

Let's Play DRUTHERS!

SO FUN!

Druthers is a game in which you are given two choices and you have to choose one. Some are fun while others are gross, but you have to choose!

For each Druther, choose your answer by checking the box by your preference.

Would you rather...

Have the ability to fly ☐

OR

Have the apiLity to be invisible ☐

Would you rather...

Live in space ☐

OR

Live deep in the sea ☐

Would you rather...

Be able to speak all human languages

☐

OR

Be able to talk to animals ☐

Would you rather...

Have a personal chef ☐

OR

Have a personal chauffeur ☐

Would you rather...

Be stuck in a rom-com

☐

OR

Be stuck in an action movie ☐

Would you rather...

Sneeze glitter

OR

Fart bubbles

☐ ☐

Would you rather...

Always be cold

OR

Always be hot

☐ ☐

Would you rather...

Eat popcorn

OR

Eat chocolate

☐ ☐

Would you rather...

Spend a day being a cat

OR

Spend a day being a dog

☐ ☐

Would you rather...

Win $10,000 for yourself

OR

Have your friend win $100,000

☐ ☐

Would you rather...

Have a pet dragon

OR

Have a pet unicorn

☐ ☐

Would you rather...

Live without internet ☐ **OR** Live without hot showers ☐

Would you rather...

Have three eyes ☐ **OR** Have three legs ☐

Would you rather...

Always be 10 minutes late ☐ **OR** Always be 20 minutes early ☐

Would you rather...

Burp every five minutes ☐ **OR** Fart every five minutes ☐

Would you rather...

Be the world's best dancer ☐ **OR** Be the world's best singer ☐

Would you rather...

Have lots of money and no friends ☐ **OR** Have lots of friends and no money ☐

I'm leaving you a list of my favorite songs and musicians because music has been part of my story, and I want you to keep listening long after I'm gone.

When one of these songs comes on, turn it up and think of me. Sing along. And please, dance. It is absolutely okay to cry and to miss me. I know there will be days when the tears need to come. But I hope there will also be days when you dance.

Close your eyes and pretend I'm right there beside you. Actually, you won't have to pretend. Even when you can't see me, I'll be there. In the music, in your memories, and in all the love we shared.

So turn it up a little louder. I'll be singing and dancing right along with you.

MY FAVORITE SONGS & MUSICIANS

These are the songs and artists that mean something to me.

On these next pages,

write a letter to your loved ones letting each of them know what you think of them how you value relationship with them.

Dear

Date:

Dear

Date:

Dear

Date:

Dear

Date:

A Letter to Me

Now write a letter to yourself.
Tell yourself how you feel right now
and how you wish things could be.
Be honest and do not be afraid to say
what you really think. ♡

Dear Me, Date: ________________

Your Self Portrait

Memories With Me

On a previous page, you asked your loved ones to describe you with one word

On these next pages, ask them to share one special memory they have with you and record their responses:

Name: ____________

My special memory with you:

____

____

____

Name: ____________

My special memory with you:

____

____

____

____

Name: ____________

My special memory with you:

____

____

____

Name: ____________

My special memory with you:

____

____

____

Thank you for sharing your memories!

Name: ______________

My special memory with you:

Name: ______________

My special memory with you:

Name: ______________

My special memory with you:

Name: ______________

My special memory with you:

Name: ______________

My special memory with you:

Name: ______________

My special memory with you:

Name: ____________

My special memory with you:

Name: ____________

My special memory with you:

Name: ____________

My special memory with you:

Name: ____________

My special memory with you:

Name: ____________

My special memory with you:

Name: ____________

My special memory with you:

Name: ______________

My special memory with you:

Name: ______________

My special memory with you:

Name: ______________

My special memory with you:

Name: ______________

My special memory with you:

Name: ______________

My special memory with you:

Name: ______________

My special memory with you:

Remember Me

Nobody lives forever. Eventually, we all have a time to be born and a time to die. Of course, we would all like to live to an old age with great health and simply fall asleep and die with no pain. Sadly, that is not the way life is for most people.

One day, you will die, and that time might be soon. This little book might just be a sweet surprise you leave behind for your loved ones so that when you are gone, they can remember you the way you'd like to be remembered.

You have written about yourself through these pages, and you have also recorded your family and friends' memories with you.

For this final section, do your best to share your heart and final thoughts about your life. How do you hope to be remembered by the people who love you?

When my time has come and I am gone,
Let not your heart feel all alone.
In whispered winds and morning dew,
You'll feel my spirit there with you.
A laugh we shared, a look, a song,
In memories, I still belong.
So light a star inside your chest,
And know I'm near, in silent rest.

Remember Me

Published by Ashland Ink Publishing
209 West 2nd Street #177
Fort Worth TX 76102
www.bellasteri.com

Published in the United States of America

ISBN: 978-1-963514-20-9

Ashland Ink is a publishing imprint under the Bell Asteri Foundation. Proceeds of book sales benefit childhood cancer research and programs and help to support the mission of Bell Asteri: to improve the lives of the children of the cancer community through the art of storytelling.

www.ingramcontent.com/pod-product-compliance
Lightning Source LLC
LaVergne TN
LVHW010737061126
851857LV00014B/1531
9798952367005